The Primordial Mind

Also by Cadeyn McLellan

Journey to the Sun
Exodus

Copyright information

Quotations taken from;
- *King James Bible*. (1973). Holman Bible Publishers. (Original work published 1611)
- *NIV Bible*. (2011). Zondervan Pub. House.
- Thomas, D. (2003). *Dylan Thomas Selected Poems, 1934-1952*. New Directions Publishing Corporation.
- Sagan, C. (1997). *Pale Blue Dot: A Vision of the Human Future in Space*. Ballantine Books. (Original work published 1994)
- Blake, W., Robinson, C., & Robinson, M. H. (2011). *Songs of Innocence*. Dover Publications.
- Theophrastus Paracelsus. (2014). *The Archidoxes of Magic*. Literary Licensing, LLC.
- Chie Kutsuwada, Appignanesi, R., & Shakespeare, W. (2009). *As you like it*. Self Made Hero.
- Plato. (n.d.). *Allegory of the Cave*.

All works quoted are in the public domain.

Cover art by Stefano B. Edied by Michael Martin. Artist photo taken by Bek Stokes. Published and distributed through Ingram Spark.

Copyright © 2025 by Cadeyn McLellan. All rights reserved. No portion of this book may be reproduced in any form without written permission from the publisher or author, except as permitted by U.S. copyright law.

ISBN: 978-1-7640159-1-2 First Edition Hardback.

Volume 2: The Primordial Mind

For my wild child, Ransom.

Introduction

When writing, I rarely considered publication. Therefore, I wrote entirely from the heart. This collection contains some of my most self-reflective poems. Like my life, they spiral up and down. Some were written in pits of grief and broken bones; others in the peaks of adrenaline and adventure.

I am often asked why I live my life in such a way. Why the extremes? Maybe these poems provide some insight, or perhaps they just serve to diagnose me. Either way, they are honest.

I am now starting to see similar traits in my little son, Ransom. I hope he finds a path with less injuries. Yet at the same time I want him to experience the same heights of joy I have felt.

Volume 2
The Primordial Mind

Volume 2: The Primordial Mind

Chapter 1: Dancing Subjects of the Embryonic Mind
1. The Venus and the Sorcerer — 2
2. Stone — 5
3. Evolution's Shadow — 6
4. Three Sonnets to Modern Man — 10

Chapter 2: All Civilization of Mind Vanquished
5. Lessons from the Coast — 16
6. Magnolia Bloom — 34

Chapter 3: The Labyrinth Walls of Mind and Will
7. The Quintessence — 38
8. Mirror Man — 50
9. Numb — 51
10. The Present — 52
11. Despair — 53
12. Streetlights — 54
13. The Dualistic Image — 57

Chapter 4: Entanglement
14. Entanglement of Souls — 60
15. Pipe Organ — 61
16. Grief — 62
17. Queen of Eden — 64
18. Familial Flowers — 66

Chapter 5: Returning to the Mythical
19. Circadian Rhythms — 72
20. Final Forms — 75
21. Beside the Fire — 78

Dancing Subjects of the Embryonic Mind

The Venus and the Sorcerer
Part I: The Cave

Deep in the warmth of the womb of the earth,
Ancient rooms heaped in stalactites.
Fossilised light flickers the wall in amber.
Her skin's grandeur flushing; crystal and marble,
Rock faces blushing and breathing.
Rushing down her arms and fingers,
Passageways through her body.
Savage animals nude and wild eyed;
Dancing subjects of the embryonic mind.
Spiralling the vortex of a virginal world,
The breath, the sex, the hunt.
Hades' beasts running, drumming,
Walls humming and vibrating by the flames dizzying.
Animalia named yet remain untamed;
All running deeper and deeper
To the plethora of bowing creatures.
Kneeling as if entombed before her temple,
Here at the Eve of creation.
Their eyes bloom desire and terror,
Eyes glowing in the flame and instinct.
Foreign now, seems that knowing fire of sensual fear,
From our distance of thirty thousand years.

The Venus and the Sorcerer
Part II: Venus

Two hands feverishly work a hanging canvas.
Veins expand, pulsating with quickness here at the zenith
Under the image of Venus.
The fire pit bleeds beneath, white as shell,
In whose embers the seeds of paradise dwell,
Figuring into the figure of a woman,
Forming the favoured features: all engulfing,
Pulsing from their author's fervour.
Charcoal thighs rise up, destination of uncertain good
Unto the black garden of her womanhood.
That single shape and sacred shade,
Such yearning inlaid, ready to burst,
Beginning thirty thousand years of thirst.
That hypnotising black triangle
Striking balance between the tribal and the beautiful.
Mystery bound to majesty: love here there may still be.
And yet.
Desire is not so easily satisfied,
Nor content to be denied merely with subtlety.
The smallest of cuts made in the stone,
In which all manner of madness enthroned.
That single cut, breathlessly, the rising blood.
Let's flood the Neolithic ecstasy,
Spinning sensual sorcery,
Beguilement and bewilderment,
Love, lust, exultation, radiation,
The dance of primal romance:
Lust descending down from hade's empyrean heights.
Pleasure isolated, precipitated, nothing left to give.
Hips rise to no ascension.
No belly, no breasts, nor heat of the heartbeat,
Nor eyes which make beauty complete:
Venus left faceless in pleasure's desolate cry.

The Venus and the Sorcerer
Part III: The Sorcerer

Out of the perverse grotesquery
Burst free a new vortex.
As spirits immersed themselves in the canvas,
Veiling Venus in a cloak of animals.
Bison and lion stroking and trailing their paws,
Down her fragmented and furtive form: shameless,
Enchanted as they become one: shapeless.
The Minotaur giving his face to Venus,
Gifting grace to the graceless tragedy.
The sorcerer weaving fig leaves,
Concealing Sheba from Solomon,
Steals away that siren symphony,
Restoring some dignity
With empathy
To her war-torn shores.
Eve lies once more with Eden's creatures,
And yet the fall still radiates with seizures.
For what was lost shall not return,
And what was done shall not be undone.
That dichotomous heart and its porous dividing walls,
Beating through unchanging evolution, creation and fall,
Love to lust in cruel dilution
Begets thirty thousand years of pollution.

Stone

Were that my life a stone within my palm,
I may reflect her fossilised patterns.
My fingers polish a living embalm,
Shaping the quartz as faces are fashioned.
The stone into something beautiful moves,
As smoothed are the veins of her crystal grooves.

    Yet such insight is only possible
    In the risk of dropping that precious stone
    To a chasm in life unreachable;
    For we're not mind alone but bound in bone.
    So as our soapstone and the flame collide,
    Like black obsidian are purified.

    As our sandstone is weathered and treasured,
        Plesiosaurus is freed of her slate.
    Through pleasure and pain our stones are measured,
        In motion sublime our amber rotates.
        Until in the end shatters like all things,
    And becomes the dust from which we did spring.

Evolution's Shadow

1

Coelacanth swims idly
In Cambrian's shadowless sea,
Her form unchanged since the dawn,
As by dusk our species was born.
The start of a dynasty,
From infinite variety,
To the brink of deities,
Transforms our pride and piety.
Breaking bones and shedding skin,
All life, as fuel, consumed within.
Death our vessel to the light,
Fins to hands, shadow black as night,
Soulless reincarnation,
Of a stronger generation.
Lowly Coelacanth laments
The wanton waste of our ascent.

Evolution's Shadow

2

Rising up on primate feet
In brutal tribal ape elite,
Conquering savannah land,
Lower beasts vanquished, tool in hand.
Pneuma and virtue laid waste,
Enslaving the primitive race,
Auctioning off tribal art,
Painted with a Coelacanth heart.
Paradise to Hades turned;
Underfoot grassland, black and burned.
As hands and minds take the reins
Of our evolution's domain,
Forging our own destiny
Over nature's ascendency.
Balance, turned to agony,
Filled by shadow's duality.

Evolution's Shadow

3
Making squares of land and sea,
Freed at last of Fibonacci,
Mother once reigned over us,
She now subdued, laid dust to dust:
Time and distance quantified
By earth no longer mystified.
Coelacanth on the menu
Of the high rise with the sea view.
The power of the atom
In our palm is but a spasm.
No new land for our green eyes,
So we look to mutate the skies,
Unbound from nature's tether,
Evolution interstellar.
Yet even up in the stars,
Shadow in the machine still mars.

Evolution's Shadow

4
Ascending into godhood,
Our ancestors are firewood
For our perfection of form
As we, to higher strength, transform.
Shoulders tearing skin like strings,
Icarus bursting forth his wings,
The Moth King, wrapped in ego,
Lusting after the sunlit glow.
As smoke and flame descended,
The flight of his wings was ended.
Yet it was shadow, not light,
That took him to eternal night,
Every form and skin we shed,
From our shadow we're never bled.
Coelacanth at last swallowed
In the shallows of man's shadow.

Three Sonnets to Modern Man
Adrenaline

O modern man so numb in slumbering,
Vicarious his life of voyaging.
He lost his name in lines of numbering,
By dusk his mind and body splintering.

Dormant within there lies a deep wellspring
That reconnects to primal odysseys:
Spiralling chaos and romance in swing
The flames of Fibonacci propelling.

Embrace the fear with mind and body one,
In facing death with an evolving form.
Instincts renewed from before time begun,
Your heartbeat chants your name in swirling storm.

Reclaiming myself in adrenaline,
Becoming consequential once again.

Three Sonnets to Modern Man
Pain

O modern man no measure or meaning,
His knight's mantra: Pursue all happiness.
Prevent all pain and pleasure all feeling,
Be gratified now instantaneous.

With pain in banishment to lands remote,
The snake is gone and we in paradise;
Yet venom hides the healing antidote
As many virtues hide within their vice.

This endless pleasure will never suffice;
To equal consequence we all are bound.
So pleasure always achieved with a price;
Yet sharing pain is where our joy is found.

Find not a life of painless innocence,
But claim a life in crucial consequence.

Three Sonnets to Modern Man
Chivalry

O modern man left purposeless in dawn,
For Mars once led Venus in cosmic dance.
Yet now the call of knighthood lies in thorns,
And now the earth it spins us out of trance.

Collective Mars, in his virtue and vice,
Has long since traded sword and honesty:
Equality yet leadership the price,
And virtue dulled into monotony.

Yet planets bloom in cosmic difference,
So reignite the kiln in starry night,
And dance again in love and reverence;
For man in leading is valor and light.

For dragons still they prey upon the free,
Vanguard against them in new chivalry.

All Civilization of Mind Vanquished

Lessons from the Coast
Burning Palms

I walked a path in autumn's breeze,
Through summer lands by restless seas.
My path unknown like vast ocean,
My way was scattered, choice in motion.
There Atlantis rose up from swell,
Before into the past she fell.
Endless stones up which to clamber,
Now ever is wrapped in amber.
This day left to reminiscence,
Fossilised in perseverance.
This path now walks just in my mind
In sweetest memory enshrined.
As mayflies live for but one day,
I shall not walk again this way.

Lessons from the Coast
Burning Palms

If I returned, then I would see
A new path there beside the sea
To break the path that walks in me,
Atlantis then a sunken key.
Even if I through some third eye
Could see myself in autumn skies,
Would I now recognise myself
Upon that continental shelf?
Would I as mist then cease to be
Inside those hills and palm marquees?
For I have long since shed that skin,
My evolution from within.
My former self now wavering,
Like wattle waving in the spring.

Lessons from the Coast
Old Coalcliff Station

By Day
Here and now I vanguard youth unbroken,
Sprawling out into the great blue open.
Venerating in brazen adventure,
My spirit which blossoms from the centre.
All civilisation of mind vanquished,
By the wild romance of stone now kissed.
Atop the edge of a dizzying fall,
Where stretches beneath the crumbling walls.
The abandoned tracks of man's ambition,
Tunnelling into a cataclysm.
A little descendant of Chernobyl,
With no more coal at the earth's bestowal.
Switchmen and whistles but a memory,
As this museum becomes moss and tree.
The distant echoes of the shunting trains,
To the birdsong all but lost and arcane,
To my Reveille her view seemed a dirge:
Untouchable here in my eagle perch.
And yet shall not my bones also splinter,
Entering with this wreck into winter?

Lessons from the Coast
Old Coalcliff Station

By Night
Here again trailing dark and aged night,
Clinging to youth like some tunnel of light.
Waiving "The Last Post," her composition,
Denying my changing disposition.
The line of victories which lay behind
Their paths consuming my body and mind:
Each in their time to me the odyssey,
In memory just island oddities.
Now seeing the station lit by the moon,
Much harder it is to sing the old tune.
Those tracks by day seemed so much more distant:
Now grows in the gloom our shared existent.
As red signals burn beyond all reason,
Except to deny nature her season.
And as my retinas redden with their glow,
My own prophecy is to me bestowed.
My youth shall *"burn and rave at close of day,"*
Through crumbled bones until my judgement day.
Though unrecognised shall go this hour,
Here and now I'll vanguard my own valour.

Lessons from the Coast
Eagle Rock

Upon seeing an unrequited sunrise and rainbow during an ultramarathon.

Running in autumn in stark moonlight,
Ambition drives me through dark of night,
Ascending each hill a brutal quest,
My heart pulsating in spartan chest,
Mind focused on and driven by pain.
No symbiosis with path or rain,
Although this path I have loved before,
Now my desire is but for war.
In love I had choice, but now one way,
As victor or vanquished the price I pay.
Yet cascading dawn, blooming on me,
Forcing me to slow,
Alone by the sea.

The Dawn
Breaking through rain and rainbow light
By the flowing and the glowing of the waterfall
Whose stream was a baptismal fountain
Under clouds like cathedrals in the mountains.
The Rock
Like an ancient God of epic intent,
Raising his wings out of eternity,
Coalescing with the crashing sea,
In the beauty of his divinity.
The Rainbow
Raising up for one picturesque moment,
Encircling the eagle and the sun,
Violet spiralling all things into one,
As everything composes to majesty.

Lessons from the Coast
Eagle Rock

Choice
To lay down arms in quiet consolation,
Of this stirring of divinity.
Or be denied in ambition of pride,
A man of lead or a man of golden sea.
Alchemy
Nothing we plan is impossible:
Descendancy and ascendancy,
As much before as rock and sea,
Shall vanity or vice fill the heart in me?
The Heart
Robbed of her feel, hardened to steel,
In stone composed and in folly raised;
Her impulsive beat, thoughtless unreal,
Suppressed by a mind that cannot be saved.

Alone by the sea.
Warm invitation
Coldly denied of her ovation.
For running I am into the sun;
My heart and folly have been made one.
Victory is more vital to me
Than that sunrise over rainbow sea,
Yet guilt within my ego is laid
To tarnish the valour I have made
The love of sunrise which I had spurned.
Now never again can I return,
For victory has become a vice,
Costing me a piece of paradise.

Lessons from the Coast
Booderee Scrub Land

Upon awaking in the scrub with no memory of myself

Warm
My form
Shimmering
Light dizzying
Soft awakening
Leaf and tree cradling
Rising to stand in the vortex
Now lost my memory's codex
Eyes open: yet no soul endowment
And yet, fearless, I breathed in the moment

Feeling as if upon sunlight swimming,
Untangled from the coils of the deep,
The sirens' treasure no longer clinging,
Pleasures for the beasts of the sea to keep.
Riding the crest of an unending wave,
No damning undertow or shore to save.

Without former regret and guilt of self,
Motionless spinning: formless and faceless,
Futurity no longer held her wealth.
Like a desert mirage I was baseless,
Without a name or claim now lingering,
Free to live here inside this twinkling.

Lessons from the Coast
Booderee Scrub Land

Every love and pain, every joy and strain,
Dropped from me like the petals from a rose.
Without memory, none of them remain:
A viceless rhyme unstuck from any prose.
A virtue-less vessel floating in space,
Yet I was filled by an elated grace.

Softening all those edges once sharpened,
Every form and shape I had once taken;
The arteries of the heart long hardened,
Here in this strange place from me were shaken.
This spiral, for the first time since my birth,
Has shed from me all my preconceived worth.

All I know is this little spinning wild,
Of dragonflies and snails revolving,
Just like in the world of the smallest child,
Before the cursed age begets evolving:
As I transfused with the rays of the sun,
My soul and eucalyptus became one.

Yet such connection is but temporal
For memories make men sentinels
And I came flooding back to me
As the vortex turned to sea
In memory downing
Myself staining me
Hope and regret
Name regained
Feeling
Cold.

Lessons from the Coast
Nelson's Beach

"When I consider thy heavens, the work of thy fingers, the moon and the stars, which thou hast ordained; What is man, that thou art mindful of him? and the son of man, that thou visitest him? For thou hast made him a little lower than the angels, and hast crowned him with glory and honour." ~ **Psalm 8**

1

A mother beholding the sinking sun,
Around whom our beautiful earth is spun.
As her son gazing at a grain of sand,
A crystal within the palm of his hand.
In splashing and flashing of sunset tides,
Waves crashing and colours cascading wide.
In the clouds ascending and descending,
Angelic forms in sunbeam suspending.
And all that swim in the paths of the sea,
All swirling and glisten in majesty.
Circadian rhythms in harmony,
And with Fibonacci a symphony
Harmonic and rhythmic in their beauty.

Lessons from the Coast
Nelson's Beach

2
And yet the earth in her beauty, I'm told,
Is within the eye of he who beholds.
For every man a-grieving in sorrow
Will find no beauty in dusk or morrow.
Then all that advances in this sunset
Must only be what my eyes can beset.
Yet still the sunrise continues to roll,
And even to places without a soul.
Earth is always sunrising, sunsetting,
For dawn and dusk are always begetting.
And even when I am lucky to see
A perfect moment just over the sea,
Even then my five senses of pleasure
Are truly insufficient to measure.
For my eyes cannot see beyond the bay,
And my ears cannot hear beyond the spray.
Weather seen by man or angels alone:
Still beauty shall ever make earth her home.
For us to behold is to be humbled,
And there our philosophy does crumble
In the crash of the waves' wash and tumble.

Lessons from the Coast
Nelson's Beach

3
Yet I'm told man is nothing but carbon,
Evolution our maker and garden.
Genetics are nothing but random chance;
Our lives are a spasm and not a dance.
Ethiopian trees, our ancient home,
Are meaningless as our ancient sea bones.
And yet too I'm told all carbon is found
In the ancient stars of the heavens bound.
So our quintessence, the essence of stars,
That our souls have maintained even thus far;
Still a piece in our hearts of cosmic storm,
In contrast to our terrestrial form.
A little sand grain of eternity
Is laid in the heart of humanity.
I cannot forever dwell in sunset,
Nor see our *"Pale Blue Dot"* in her fret.
And yet, here I again, on turquoise shores,
Amazed again like so often before.
For beauty sublime is enough for me,
That conscious thought leads me back to the sea
Against evolution's trajectory.

Lessons from the Coast
Nelson's Beach

4

The *"Pale Blue Dot"* in her majesty
The quintessence of life for those who see:
For sublimity and divinity,
Clamber in sunrise and set in the sea.
And the earth between, she glitters like gold,
Bestowing to those who stand and behold
In the sun and the moon in trance and dance,
As creatures in tune fill up the expanse.
For the beauty of the cosmos is true
And lies in the heart of ancient and new;
And in every creature in every land,
In a mother's life which glows and expands,
And the grain of sand in the baby's hand.

Lessons from the Coast
Greenfields Rock Shelf

A thousand times I wandered by these stones,
As summer climbs her way through winter's bones:
To be immersed in ocean energy,
Yet not reversed to see the synergy.
The tides and waves in their hypnotic storm
Which hides away all nature's other forms.
Yet just behind the sunset of the sea:
A beauty yet to be consigned to me.

A thousand years of etching waterfalls,
In this frontier embellished by the squalls.
In spirals, fossils, water wells and light,
Form deep puzzles of shell and stalactite.
Sand reemerges from the Triassic,
As sunset submerges in soft magic.
And as moonlight lines the outcrop in night,
My heart attuned to a sublimer sight.

As bioluminescence does amaze,
Yet rocky coalescence has no praise.
For these beholding eyes are so faulty,
Which need an unfolding to see beauty.
For beauty belongs to all of the earth,
The sea and her songs, the stones of her worth.
Within this shelf is an infinitude,
Of nature's golden wealth sublime and nude.

Lessons from the Coast
Whiting Beach Waterfall

Lying by the sea,
Covered by purple clouded paradise,
Coiled vice-less like an ammonite
Behind the wall of a waterfall,
Transfixed by the transmutation.
At the brightening end of the rain's journey
Of water into sandy destination,
Cycling up from cloudy sea,
And rolling back down to me.
The verging and curtaining of the water:
Salt and fresh, merging and surging.
There transfusing
And slowly moving
Back into the sea,
Back into the sea.

Lessons from the Coast
Whiting Beach Waterfall

The in-between world of stone and sand and sea,
Where waves wash the rocks
With their turquoise touch;
The side of stone smoothed by splashing noise
The shaping of ceaseless timeless tides,
Softening and blossoming.
Creation continuing by schools of fish jostling.
New grains of sand weighed down,
Shaded dunes dancing down,
As waves cascade down,
Waterfall-ing down,
Here in the in-between,
Here in the in-between.

Lessons from the Coast
Whiting Beach Waterfall

Over the calm blue sheen and distant green,
Floral fingers gleaming wet,
These lush green ferns a rising steeple,
Around the parabolas of this citadel.
Dwelling people-less heaped in solitude,
Imbued in nature wild and nude,
No sound within but for bird hymns.
Echoing above the eyes of a solitary seal,
Who lies upon the rock to feel the waves mellowing.
As the waterfall, colouring all, watching all, mending all,
Transcending and descending down,
Sending all light bending around,
In the greens and the blues,
In the greens and the blues.

Lessons from the Coast
Whiting Beach Waterfall

Humanity falls into a distant memory
In the walls of this waterfall,
Spinning a vernal vortex as rays beset
This shelter of sunset.
As springs weltering storms
Distil their forms in distant rain
Into the heat of summer slumber,
Gentle dripping drops in number.
Season bound and solace found;
Flawlessly changing and hanging beauty,
That only the lonely molluscs see.
Under marquees of banksia trees,
This beach of plenty,
Tides fill and empty,
This far from humanity,
This far from humanity.

Lessons from the Coast
Whiting Beach Waterfall

Gazing through the water sublime,
I sort a metaphor for the waterfall,
A simile to slip into the sea.
Some deeper poetry to sing with the birds in the trees,
A lesson to impart in the heart of me.
Porous stones to synthesise
With my own soul.
Some verse of mystery
To make this poem feel more whole.
But here in the sublimity of the sea
None came to me.
So, I let go what language knows,
And let flow the soul, for
This water is sublime enough,
This water is sublime enough.

Magnolia Bloom

Her flowers bursting in sincerity,
And how fragile her beauty, petaled pink.
Each bloom a ring of happy memory,
As winter melodies begin to sink.

Within her spiralling complexity,
There is a heart of pure innocence,
Which to the bees is yearly charity,
But guilt to me is in our difference.

For in her form is sweet transparency,
A life so free of disparate contempt.
Her blooms are happy in their brevity,
And yet I with the world am not content.

If I could rebirth as her sapling child,
Could she then tame my hubris, dark and wild?

The Labyrinth Walls of Mind and Will

The Quintessence
Part I: Navigation of the Heart

1
Often it is said to me
That love indwells us peacefully:
Whispering of wings therein,
The wellspring of the heart within.
Happiness and the sublime:
The human soul our holy shrine.
The pursuit of happiness,
A pleasure instantaneous;
Human heart a vessel true,
In which all darkness is subdued.
So I choose to journey in,
Through deepest walls of heart within.
Scales and a feather held
To see what in my heart indwells.

2
Gardens green and flowers stand,
All cut and pruned by human hands.
Rows and columns outward face,
And no decay within this place.
Roses bloomed and thorns were worn,
Perfected forms with nothing torn
In expression sweet and warm,
And bioluminescent forms.
Neat and tidy pleasantries,
These boarder lands that men can see.
Made for strangers to be sweet,
Society and heart do meet.
It ironically invites,
Yet build to thwart a deeper sight.

The Quintessence
Part I: Navigation of the Heart

3
Leaving gardens far behind
To find unfiltered heart and mind
Over moss-laid garden walls,
A labyrinth laid out long and tall.
Garden veins had made their way,
Some colour in the desert grey.
Thistles grew more commonly,
The flowers now a rarity.
Sand was stirred inside the soil,
Where tracks of vipers made their coil.
Ruins dot the desert sky,
These shadowlands that never tried.
Thoughts, emotions tangled here:
My conscience dangling in fear.

4
Soon the land had nothing whole:
The wastelands of the human soul.
Sand gave way to swamp and marsh;
In mud and islands fauna sparse.
Channels maze their way through hills:
The labyrinth walls of mind and will.
Bastions small of charity,
In seas of selfish odysseys.
Blessing, cursing, love and scorn:
Dualistically, my mind is torn,
Nihilism there in me
With love and positivity.
Wading through the bog and filth
In search of soil rich and tilth.

The Quintessence
Part I: Navigation of the Heart

5
Yet the richness did not come;
A place I came of things undone.
Skeletons were all the trees,
With so few leaves and all diseased.
In eternal winter lost,
Mosaic splinters in the frost.
Good intentions withering,
Temptation's voice is whispering.
Hopes of youth have given way
To cold experiential sway.
Sins and failures hidden here,
In taught behaviour's cold veneer.
Sorrowful my heart became,
Inside this land of buried shame.

6
Then I came to labyrinth stones,
Whose centre held my heart enthroned.
Hopeful pride my mapping cord,
With innocence as my broadsword.
On the walls my past was laid,
For which my heart was to be weighed.
Turn by turn, with growing fear,
My sword grew rust as past laid clear.
Every good deed on the walls,
And every time I did not fall.
Yet the chaos also carved
Addictions deep and goodness starved.
I stepped forth into the dark,
Morality by choice made stark.

The Quintessence
Part I: Navigation of the Heart

7
Sacrifice on floors within,
The vestal virgins paid my sin.
Walls gave way to beast and core,
In fear my sword and map no more.
In a flash of horns and hooves,
And trapped in fur: I could not move.
Then my chest was torn in two,
My heart through abdomen removed.
And upon the scales placed,
My heart a failure without grace.
Then the beast turned into me
In dark familiarity.
Both our hearts had been unsown;
For in this place, I was alone.

8
Shaking myself from that place,
For no more torture I could face.
In my heart I sought for wealth,
But found instead my shadow self.
Most men know their quality,
Yet hide their deep iniquity.
If explored with honesty,
The heart of darkness you will see.
Joy will not be found within,
For pride is crushed in weight of sin.
Wisdom was my journey's end,
Along the way I lost a friend.
The desire it impressed:
To know myself a little less.

The Quintessence
Part II: Navigation of the Mind

1
Teachers often say to me,
The mind of man wills destiny.
Evolution of our thought,
Our species from primeval wrought.
Social education wise,
Our adaptation's holy guise.
Though all chaos may descend,
To heaven's lights our minds ascend.
So I chose to journey through,
My mind to find the false and true.
Looking for that touch divine,
That flame and spark that gave us mind.
Following Prometheus,
To beauty find or hideous.

2
In reverse through mind and eye,
I fell through smoke of city sky.
Cluttering metropolis:
Immediate my consciousness.
Thoughts in millions all advance,
Chaotic pulsing circumstance.
Liquid flames in neon hue:
By time my mind is torn in two.
The empty and trivial
On daily anvils jovial.
Evolution's deeper thought
Is from these buildings rarely wrought.
Hard, so hard, to see the sun,
And hardest to keep mind as one.

The Quintessence
Part II: Navigation of the Mind

3
Out from crowd and concrete I,
Did walk to town of beach and sky.
Suits to children soon became,
As thoughts did slow to social games.
Making castles out of sand,
In compromise to other's hands.
Cultured words in custom's voice,
And history informs all choice.
Moulding mind like muddy clay,
As will is formed like tidal bays.
Social movements shepherd sheep;
Our minds go easily to sleep.
Goosestepping shadow from light,
As justice hollowed into night.

4
Sharing will is compromise,
The social realm of truth and lies.
So I sought for solitude
On desert roads so long eschewed,
Seeking to ascend the land
Through countless paths in wining sands.
Always choice ahead of me,
Unhindered by anxiety.
For in youth my will was strong,
Yet by the night my way gone wrong.
Temptation arose like dunes,
No one to keep me from her tune.
Hardship long I can endure,
But for my shadow self no cure.

The Quintessence
Part II: Navigation of the Mind

5
Standing there in schism dark,
In desert sand dualism stark.
An oasis to my left,
Where creativity is blessed.
Where these very words found form,
As order stilled from chaos storm.
Planting date palms aqueducts,
As Petra's poetry instructs.
Yet to right stand jackals cold,
My shadow self from Babel old.
In his desolater smile,
My words confused all turn to bile.
In creation chaos glued:
Ascension, not in solitude.

6
Each ascent found in my mind,
Was bound to a descent in kind.
So I sought for ancient lands,
Where first did fire grace our hands.
Downwards through the glacial caves,
To find first man of ancient days.
All his stories paint the stone,
A beautiful and savage throne.
Distant narrative within,
Yet hunting art was strangely kin.
Echoing from deepest cave,
I entered in my mind to brave.
Hunched in form Cro-Magnon man,
Prometheus, two sticks in hand.

The Quintessence
Part II: Navigation of the Mind

7
Then a spark did glint his eyes,
Until ascending flames did rise.
Dance enchanted flaming night,
Decanting shadow and the light.
Flames then made me visible,
Our eyes met through the mythical.
Fearful eyes as blue as mine,
Identical our minds' design.
With his sacrificial knife,
He tore my liver in delight.
As my abdomen was bled,
The veil of our difference shed.
Knife and liver in my hand,
Alone inside this cave I stand.

8
Fled in fear through mind and eye,
As my hope in ascension died.
Evolution of our mind,
Yet no less human in design.
Social games and dancing flames,
Our poetry in cave remains.
Light and shadow day and night,
So little change within our plight.
Our ascension never whole,
Our minds descension in our souls.
From the flame so little gleamed,
Prometheus is unredeemed.
Hopeless is the heart and mind,
For unperfected is our kind.

The Quintessence
Part III: Navigation of the Soul

1
Of the soul philosophy
Does speak without consistency.
Some ascribe the spiritual
To their emotions' rituals,
Yet denying it a place
In the toils of our race.
Others disbelieving say,
We are but soulless DNA.
Measuring in present tense,
The soul is but what we can sense.
Time and substance left behind,
I sought to find this soul of mine.
Sailing Styx that river dark,
To death itself so cold and stark.

2
Autoscopy taking me,
To view the mind and body free.
Outside of myself I stood,
By meditating amber hoods.
Thoughtless chanting, wordless song,
That jealous to the soul belong:
Without pain and pleasureless,
In their existence weightlessness.
Soul ascent enlightenment,
Through nothingness escape descent.
In Nirvana bodiless,
Our souls by purgatory blessed.
This life seemed like suicide,
So I found life of soul denied.

The Quintessence
Part III: Navigation of the Soul

3
In a brothel I awoke
In atheist apostle yoke.
There I sought impurity,
Salaciously in vanity.
Watching as the bodies writhe,
My spirit swallowed in demise.
Took to every spirit wine,
And every siren I made mine.
Guilt addiction day and night,
Grotesquely grew my appetite.
Though I pleasured every whim,
My soul was not content within.
Monks and whores disparity:
In Styx is solidarity.

4
Two lives had I thus observed.
These guides down Styx I could not serve,
So I sought out death to find,
Where soul and body there do bind
With two ladies, old as stone,
Awaiting for their graves alone.
One to whom life had been drained,
Into something complete deigned.
Moments of her clarity,
Make such sadness of rarity.
Spirit barely holding grip,
Upon the river soon to slip.
Progeny made premature,
Her essence death had lost, obscured.

The Quintessence
Part III: Navigation of the Soul

5
Yet a life still bloomed inside
The other whom I sat beside.
Soul alive in form undone:
Her life still full with sands now run.
Though she stood at Hades' gate,
To Styx had not resigned her fate.
Showing me how to be whole,
Her interplay of mind and soul.
In her body faltering,
Her essence still was prospering.
And in death my friends soon fell,
In death divorced what life indwelled.
Death for one was a relief,
And for the other sorrow, grief.

6
Only death that greatest sting
Could so divide the soul I cling.
So to see the mystery,
I sailed Styx's end to see.
There in death in humble show,
My form so proud now laid so low.
Body once a vessel bold,
Now sinking in the waters cold.
Laying on my windowsill,
An hourglass so nearly still,
Inscribed by the one I love;
Our souls in spirit stars above.
Youthful words so hollow now,
As Thanatos now makes me bow.

The Quintessence
Part III: Navigation of the Soul

7
Breath was coughing with decay,
To Styx my blackened heart gave way.
Then I saw so hideous,
Great Thanatos insidious.
Soul and body ripped apart,
His scythe divides my mind and heart.
And I saw no soul ascend,
Nirvana surely not the end.
Pneuma lies in breath and heart,
For only spectres live apart.
Progeny by Styx's flow,
All soon forget the soul they know.
My quintessence laid to waste,
As death and grief are interlaced.

8
Shaking myself from that grief,
I turned with truth to youth's relief.
Man is heart and mind and soul,
But flesh is that which makes them whole.
So live not in piety,
Nor senseless sensuality.
We are stardust bound to earth;
In earthly forms we find our worth.
From therein is death and sting,
Which kills quintessence everything.
Styx shall overtake us all,
Nirvana but a spectre's call.
Resurrection of the soul,
Our only hope in Styx's toll.

Mirror Man

Man of dust	Man of stone
Salt and sand	Line and edge
Pulling rust	Form is known
From my hands	Sword and pledge
Love is hard	Fortitude
To impart	Wedding rings
Tearing shards	Heart subdued
From my heart	As she sings
Lust at home	Over lands,
In winter	Desolate.
And my bones	Seeds in hand,
Which splinter	Recreate.
Soon shapeless	Courage found
Wave crumbles	Heart of flesh
Form porous	Now unbound
Mind tumbles	From regress
Misty dross	Virtue filled
In my eyes	Viceless soon
Image lost	Sun instilled
Insight dies	Banished moon
Scattered tides	Over seas
Move my thoughts	Choice and will
Thorny sides	Odysseys
Wrapped and wrought	Could not kill
Man of dusk	Man of dawn
Fading light	Form of day
Empty husk	Sword is drawn
Fearing night	Come what may

Numb

The equatorial sun,
Beaming through the canopy
Of the mossy trunks and fern:
All life alimentary.
The blooms of a vernal world
Breathing the earth's energy
In the colobus forests
Of some long ancient memory.

Now just colours past recall
Where tundra stretches empty
Into the wastelands of time.
For sojourned I a century,
With no game, no hunt, no fill,
This land elementary
Becoming the cursed blue ice
Of losing an identity.

Black beaches and short dark days,
Midnight sun and frozen sea,
A wet maze of grey and white
Where man has no supremacy.
Here where the ice spectres glide,
Slipping my mind's drudgery,
Where the past fails to warm
And pain no longer sensory.

The Present

Through the fray we spectres glide,
In permanence we don't reside.
Personal our odysseys
As we move through uncertain seas.
Each to his own siren song:
To murky depths we all belong.

    With one hand we reach behind,
    Clinging unto a fading shrine;
    Brick by brick dismantling,
    As mist does blind, so maddening.
    Dropping every sacred stone,
    Wherein the jungle claims her throne.

        One hand reaching blind ahead,
        In hope naive and fearful dread.
        A distant horizon there,
        But over waves we can but stare.
        Centred here, trapped in-between,
        The sun and moon in twilight scene.

            In rare moments of magic,
            When we are stilled from our panic,
            Wisdom grants us her insight
            In sweetest moments of hindsight.
            Yet these moments rarity,
            Keep us blind in tragedy.

Despair

Despair.
A mind of despair leaves nought full or fair,
Despair.
Through the citadel like an infidel,
As vagabonds dwell making home in hell,
Despair.
All become shapeless, formless and faceless,
Where even beauty fails to move me,
Accursed sorrow; night without morrow,
Despair.
The heart left hollow in her wallowing,
And thoughts left shallow in dark shadowing,
Better burn angry, full of zealotry,
Then be sadness drunk and shipwrecked and sunk,
Despair.
Save me pen and page; restore me some rage,
Let this dark schism and narcissism
Become a motion of any notion,
But cast stagnation into damnation,
Mind free of despair, in poetry fair.

Streetlights

1

Five accursed amber lights,
Five spectres all immersed in night
Beaming down my darkest roads.
Screaming they point in yellow robes
To a place I cannot go,
A graceless isolation row.
In the cold, my heart shivers
In fear upon the black river.
In their blinding orange blaze,
Five spectres watch man's evil ways.

2

Five lights flicker and combine,
Five demons splintering my mind,
Haunting my morality
And taunting in dark fantasies.
Temptation beats like a drum,
My anger burning fierce and numb.
Lost in rage and agony,
As blood becomes an ecstasy.
Still the drum pounds on and on,
And soon I will to them belong.

Streetlights

3
Five lights hover hell and home,
Five jackals of metallic bone.
Radiance of amber glow,
And sacrificial blood to flow.
Their voices of hate and love:
My choice to make them one with blood.
Their talons are in my veins:
My mind wanders their dark domain.
Metal hands and flood water
Calling love to make a slaughter.

4
Five lights of sorrow and grief,
Five gods of dark pagan belief.
Spires made from hate and lust,
Their metal wires, stone and dust.
Love and grace the gods deny,
In chanting sacrificial cries.
Temples in the jungle ferns:
And there atop five torches burn.
The priest and the people stare:
My heart thrown down the temple stairs.

Streetlights

5

Five lights stark inside the storm,
Five beasts of dark unearthly forms
Calling me to make a turn,
To make that fall and world to burn.
The last pleasure left in love,
In my measure of rage and blood:
It is done! Five bullets scream
As love becomes something obscene.
Five streetlights look on cruelly
Inside that flood of agony.

The Dualistic Image

A Response to Blake's "Divine Image"

To Mercy, Pity, Peace, and Love,
Few pray in their distress.
Petitioning virtues above,
And few with thankfulness.

For Mercy, Pity, Peace, and Love,
Are true names for the Lord.
And these four virtues from above,
Are right to be adored.

For darkness in the human heart,
Clouds our will and virtue.
Malice and mercy both take part,
In Christian, Turk and Jew.

Yet blazing light of God's true face
Is stark comparison.
For our chaotic backward race,
Our cancer's medicine.

Our virtue, vice and dualism,
God sees preeminent.
Our sin does form a great chasm,
Yet prays with arrogance.

Entanglement

Entanglement of Souls

An elegy for Nana

A solo voice lifting like mist,
Ascending cold the marble midst.
As soft rain patters on a rose,
In heavy weight of grief impose.
For everyone is here but one,
For whom her mission *"It is done."*
She now ascends beyond the sea,
On eagle's wings' eternity.

And yet my joy in sorrow sails,
As fog in dawn of spring does veil.
And as I speak of memory,
A twin emotion wells in me
Despite that fact that all is well.
Inside entanglement we dwell
And now a precious soul has left,
Until the end of time bereft.

My tears of loneliness and loss
Shall fall upon the empty cross
And transform to a joyful thing,
For death and sorrow have no sting.
And upward through the ceiling see
The saints in chorus majesty.
All glowing in the dawning Sun,
"Well done my faithful servant, come."

Pipe Organ

An elegy for Grampa

So softly through my childhood days,
A pipe organ in tune did play.
The lyrics laid with family
In words of faith and majesty.
I had assumed a permanence,
Yet faltering in present tense,
As whispered notes all fall to fray,
As final notes soon melt away.

What should be timeless now is lost
In silence, grief and empty loss.
If through the sorrow you can lift,
Inside this grief there is a gift.
To take your eyes over the sea,
To hear a tune at last set free.
And those of faith join in song,
To Him to whom we all belong.

And now on wings the organ sings
In verse like flowers new in spring.
For pain and sleep no longer keep
The power of the song to sweep
The hills of the eternal realms,
Where life in death no longer whelms.
The dawning sun his faith has won,
His song praising the Holy One.

Grief

I think grief is my favourite emotion,
For naught much else so stirs my soul to motion
Than the savage bite of a eulogy,
Which churns my soul up like a turbulent sea.
Her water and gravity none deny;
For her weight is by our own love supplied
And through all our tears the world is clarified.

    My happiness so fleeting unsustained,
    As summer green by the autumn red is stained
    And bought so easily with gluttony
    In the siren song of our society.
    Happiness but a shadow in shallows,
    Yet grief so deep in contrast is hallowed;
    Just as in the Shroud of Turin's afterglow.

        Melancholia sweetly sings to me
        As I witness winter strip away the trees.
        And yet still in her introspective form
        To me she is but a minor chill or warm.
        But in my heart I long for something more;
        For these cold meditations do not restore,
        Nor point me to a summer forevermore.

Grief

Guilt and grief two similar wells within
For in both the sweet and sour dwell therein.
Both agonising for the fallen way,
Both their waters aching for those awful days.
And yet guilt cycling itself does flow,
And therefore with every taste the sour grows.
And yet with each cup of grief more truth does show.

    Our grief a seed of that most ancient tree
    Of the knowledge of our own fragility.
    Under another tree we once had dwelled,
    In our lives eternal emotions we held.
    Yet now our cells all tear themselves apart,
    Eternity weighted upon our mortal hearts.
    Yet grief cries out that life should never depart.

        And then within the twinkling of an eye,
        Our grief shall transform like the bright dawning sky.
        Into an emotion completely new,
        Which Peter upon those risen shores well knew.
        Our grief a foretaste of when death destroyed,
        From our sea-bound sorrow to a sun filled joy.
        With our eternal emotion to enjoy.

Queen of Eden
Part I: Atlantis

From precious garden of my memories
We walked with hand in hand under the trees.
Eve. Singing there beside a thornless rose,
And naming countless creatures in her care.
And I living in innocent repose,
In aimless dreams upon a gentle beach.
When the foundations of the earth were new,
With endless love the swells we could subdue.

> Poets speak
> Of love's first moments burst between two hearts,
> To say they are the zenith of the art.

Upon the waters of Atlantis' coast,
I knelt before my love with rings and hope.
Eve like a rose was slowly blossoming;
In twirls and spins she bloomed before my eyes.
And I in ignorance was promising;
That light would ever grace our Eden skies.
But Eden had a path unto the past,
Where amber streetlights lit an hourglass.

> The Past moves
> A wave concaving through the present tense,
> Her torment and her joy they breathe immense.

We were unfamiliar with futility
With rings to bind us to futurity.
Eve. Down that road she now in sorrow turned,
And whispered name of Babylon with tears.
And I with Eden now all black and burned,
In fear I watched Atlantis disappear.
The hourglass a price that must be paid,
As innocence to desecration laid.

Queen of Eden
Part II: Babylon

Two children lost in lands of Babylon,
With hand in hand and nowhere to belong.
Eve. Such fragile beauty in her suffering,
In quivering and facing choices stark.
And I now know the weight of wedding rings,
Clinging to Eden's sun in twilight dark.
Wiping salty tears from her pale face,
As she subdued my restless mind to grace

> Jesus wept;
> The heart she breaks and aches and beats so brief,
> For love is sacrifice and love is grief.

At last we stood by windows Eden stained,
In sun and love at last now unrestrained.
Eve. Walking down in thornless majesty,
The isle lit by face of laughing eyes.
And I was overwhelmed by gravity,
As children now reclaimed Atlantis' skies.
In Babylon we claimed our victory,
Our love no longer wrapped in mystery.

> Time rolls on
> The power of the hourglass no more,
> Once drowning souls now crowning pristine shores.

Our days now live upon receding tides;
We pave a garden citadel inside.
Eve still loves all the creatures in her reach,
A mother truly giving love to all.
And I now dream of children on this beach.
For them Atlantis could be home to call.
From pain to beauty Eden now indwells,
With sounds of children dancing in the swell.

Familial Flowers
Night Blooming Cereus

By a desert moon a flower in bloom,
Bringing colour to a landscape of dunes.
Stretching forth beauty in utility,
And strength against nature's hostility.
Working by starlight with calming insight,
Ever-working good in her children's plight.
By day retreating to thoughtful solace,
From the care she laboured so tireless.
And I, with a belly full of nectar,
Rejoice that I was raised by no other.

Familial Flowers
Ghost Orchid

A mystery to me I am afraid;
For in this orchid not all is displayed.
Although I see her creativity,
In her petals bright and sharp filigree,
To the very few is all revealed:
Those who journey through leaves that conceal,
Where in labyrinth walls her pollen is blessed,
Earned by moths who patiently acquiesce.
The depth of relationship earned by time,
As evolution shaping those entwined.

Familial Flowers
Black Violet

These black petals I see with clarity:
In their likeness my better self I see.
Those stamens of bright yellow energy,
Beckoning her love's wide intensity.
Yet that violet in vibrant complexion,
Sadly makes me the darker reflection;
For she shares her nectar with all creatures.
I sadly lack these generous features.
A mirror we are like a lake to stars,
Yet her evolution outruns mine by far.

Returning to the Mythical

Circadian Rhythms

1

Again my form awoken to the call of dawn,
As moon and night are slipping through the fig and thorns.
Upon the earth a polyrhythm oscillates
As all her creatures chime the bells that innovate;
As if the earth in orchestra had taken form,
And made her tune between the tides and rolling storms.
We all are guided by a thousand melodies
To daily life in all her work and destiny.
And to that beat in all her pleasantries enslaved,
A daily drum and circle that we all must brave.
A figure eight on which we all are spiralling
Repeats again our twelve labours like puppet string.

Circadian Rhythms

2

A man I knew whose song was work until sundown,
So long ago he turned his rhythm to the ground.
A figure eight without any ascendency,
Abound to desert waves without a drop of sea.
As every opportunity is lost to song
Which sings to dig the dirt until you there belong.
His life in tune with those who gave up being free,
Who dwell alone and find their joy in memory.
In days when they would raise their eyes unto the sky,
Now spire-less without a flame to classify.
A middle-class Prometheus upon his rock,
From nine to five so comfortable with eagle clock.

Circadian Rhythms

3

Inside new song, awaken sleeper to thyself,
And see the world thy lost in the pursuit of wealth.
The true sunlight thou traded for a neon night,
For Eden's work found rest in cool of day so bright.
For once we worked in melody and harmony,
Our work and rest so flowed without economy.
For in creation is our reclamation won,
So raise your eyes again towards the blazing sun.
For every man in figure eight eternal swings,
But choice is ours to do so with or without wings.
And breaking free of every pointless odyssey,
To daily claim that one moment of ecstasy.

Final Forms

1

Evolution, death and birth,
The shifting forms of life on earth,
Two by two in bodies new,
A generational debut.
Through primeval pain we wrought,
The membrane of our conscious thought;
Pain and death immutable
In evolution's crucible.
Death our flaming enemy,
Tinder forms incendiary,
Without pain extinction reigns:
We are but fossils in the rain.

Final Forms

2

Every cell disintegrates,
And each vestige is laid to waste;
And yet still we beat the drum
That echoes numb beneath our lungs.
Somehow not resigned to fate,
We scratch our forms upon the slate
Through the epochs of the earth,
Man carving out temporal worth.
In our countless histories
Contending death's supremacy:
No immortal solution;
A tempest without conclusion.

Final Forms

3
Yet an answer will be found.
In time reversed our forms unbound.
Natural turns miracle,
Returning to the mythical.
Hearts shall beat among the trees,
With new aortic arteries.
In bioluminescence,
Our forms acquire quintessence.
No pain left to medicate,
Our cells ever regenerate.
Final forms then flourishing
In earth, burgeoning and blushing.

Beside the Fire

Let us sit beside the fire,
Where words become angelic spires.
Let metaphors form in the sparks,
That we may ascend to heaven's arc.
Sing again those ancient mantras,
To stave off the wolves and enchanters.
"In the beginning was the word,"
And in word evolution is heard.
Now orate the ancient lesson:
Awaken, sleeper! Learn to listen.

Let us rename all the creatures,
Beyond their scientific features;
Not debased to utility,
But reclothed in fear and majesty.
Once we roamed the realm of mammoth,
From garden sublime and first sabbath.
"And so man is their quintessence,"
For earthly fear is cosmic essence.
Not the docile eyes of the herd,
But found where leviathan is stirred.

Let us put footprints on the sand,
As little children printing their hands,
Forging our path by great ocean,
Hypnotized by eternal motion.
For dancing tides do so much more
Than scatter the sand along the shore.
Their flow the stage for odysseys
Moving in their own philosophies.
Drawn upon her surging breakers,
"The world's a stage; And we the players."

Beside the Fire

Let us try to number the stars,
And re-commune with Venus and Mars.
No telescope or microscope,
But let stories of stars be evoked.
Although we have split the atom
And looked across the cosmic chasm
Beyond the scientific proof,
"Life an enfoldment" of deeper truth.
There's greater things than galaxies,
Smaller things than atomic debris.

Let us walk out into the dawn,
"Bewilderments of the eyes" be torn
As shadowy forms flee like night,
Ascending the rise of truth and sight:
A broadsword of reclamation
Under the Sun's blazing narration.
And every splintered media,
Silenced before the Ecclesia.
In the luminance of true form,
Let us then to that fire conform.

www.ingramcontent.com/pod-product-compliance
Lightning Source LLC
Chambersburg PA
CBHW041309240426
43661CB00045B/1494/J